ROUGH TRADES

Also by Charles Bernstein:

The Absent Father in Dumbo (Zasterle, 1990)
The Nude Formalism, with Susan Bee (Sun & Moon Press, 1989)
Four Poems (Chax Press, 1988)
The Sophist (Sun & Moon Press, 1987)
Artifice of Absorption (*Paper Air*, 1987)
Veil (Xexoxial Editions, 1987)
Content's Dream: Essays 1975-1984 (Sun & Moon Press, 1985)
Resistance (Awede Press, 1983)
Islets/Irritations (Jordan Davies, 1983)
Stigma (Station Hill Press, 1981)
The Occurrence of Tune, with Susan Bee [Laufer]
    (Segue Books, 1981)
Disfrutes (Potes and Poets Press, 1981)
Controlling Interests (Roof Books, 1980)
Legend, with Bruce Andrews, Ray DiPalma,
    Steve McCaffery, and Ron Silliman
    (L=A=N=G=U=A=G=E/Segue, 1980)
Senses of Responsibility (Tuumba Press, 1979)
Poetic Justice (Pod Books, 1979)
Shade (Sun & Moon Press, 1978)
Parsing (Asylum's Press, 1976)

Editor
The Politics of Poetic Form: Poetry and Public Policy
    (Roof Books, 1990)
43 Poets (1984) (*boundary 2*, 1986)
The L=A=N=G=U=A=G=E Book, with Bruce Andrews
  (Southern Illinois University Press, 1984)
"Language Sampler" (*The Paris Review*, 1982)
L=A=N=G=U=A=G=E, with Bruce Andrews (1978-1981)

ROUGH TRADES

CHARLES BERNSTEIN

For Bill — 25 Feb[...]
Charles

SUN & MOON CLASSICS: 14

SUN & MOON PRESS
Los Angeles

Sun & Moon Press
A Program of
The Contemporary Arts Educational Project, Inc.
a non-profit corporation
6148 Wilshire Boulevard, Los Angeles, California 90048

First published by Sun & Moon Press in 1991

10 9 8 7 6 5 4 3 2 1
FIRST EDITION

Parts of this book originally appeared in *Archive for New Poetry Newsletter, Black Mountain II Review, boundary 2, The Carrionflower Writ, Central Park, Conjunctions, First Offence, Fly-by-Night Broadsides, Gandhabba, Human Means, Jimmy and Lucy's House of "K," The Line in Postmodern Poetry: A Symposium, New American Writing, The noospaper, Notus, NRG, O.blek, Poetics Statements for the New Poetics Colloquium, Poetry Project Newsletter, Raddle Moon, ReThinking Marxism, Sink, Sulfur, Talisman, Talus, Temblor, Transcendental Desktop, Up Late: American Poetry Since 1970,* and *Writing.*
"Targets of Opportunity" is reprinted from *Four Poems*
(Tucson: Chax Press, 1988)
with permission from the publisher

Copyright © Charles Bernstein, 1991
Biographical information © Sun & Moon Press, 1991
All rights reserved

Cover: *My Valentine*, by Susan Bee

LIBRARY OF CONGRESS CATALOGING IN PUBLICATION DATA
Bernstein, Charles (1950)
Rough Trades
Charles Bernstein
p. cm
ISBN: 1-55713-080-9
I. Title
811'.54   89-085480
Sun & Moon Classics: 14

Printed in the United States of America

Without limiting the rights under copyright reserved here, no part of this publication may be reproduced, stored in or introduced into a retrieval system, or transmitted, in any form or by any means (electronic, mechanical, photocopying, recording or otherwise), without the prior written permission of both the copyright owner and the above publisher of the book.

CONTENTS

The Riddle of the Fat Faced Man

The Kiwi Bird in the Kiwi Tree	11
"We Sell Ice Picks, Don't We?"	12
Precisely and Moreover	13
Riddle of the Fat Faced Man	14
Getting Wise to the Wherefores	15
Sites of Involvement	17
Nina's Party at Judy's Gym	18
Epiphanies of Suppression (3)	19
How to Disappear	21
Saltmines Regained	22
Rowing with One Oar	23
Targets of Opportunity	24
Whose Language	25
Verdi and Postmodernism	26

Rough Trades

Being a Statement on Poetics . . .	29
Reading the Tree: 1 and 2	31
Of Time and the Line	42
Wait	44
House of Formaldehyde	46
Weather Permitting	48
Force of Feeling	50
The Puritan Ethic and the Spirit of Capitalization	51
Filed Report	53
The Poet from Another Planet	56

Foam Post	58
Riot at 111 Station	60
Seven for Aotearoa	61
Slowed Reason	65
Beyond the Valley of the Sophist	67

The Persistence of Persistence

Fear of Flipping	75
Pockets of Lime	80
Blow-Me-Down Etude	89

the trades are rough
& the tide is out

THE RIDDLE OF THE FAT FACED MAN

THE KIWI BIRD IN THE KIWI TREE

I want no paradise only to be
drenched in the downpour of words, fecund
with tropicality. Fundament be-
yond relation, less 'real' than made, as arms
surround a baby's gurgling: encir-
cling mesh pronounces its promise (not bars
that pinion, notes that ply). The tailor tells
of other tolls, the seam that binds, the trim,
the waste. & having spelled these names, move on
to toys or talcums, skates & scores. Only
the imaginary is real—not trumps
beclouding the mind's acrobatic vers-
ions. The first fact is the social body,
one from another, nor needs no other.

"WE SELL ICE PICKS, DON'T WE?"

Spring fell off, like a mote inside a
lock. "I'm please you took." Therefore, or
therefrom, bumptious in material exhaustion,
mannered, as a hair might harm a
hush. There is no quiet like the
flounce of the bored, gnomed sea; no
magic like the evanescence of befuddlement
before a wand-weary song. Be a fool, &
are arcade, shut slants of light, motive
having crawled, & tusk tubes, moreover
limned with screws, hailed as hammered
pinnacle, deputized to fall. Have
leering crusts bid scowls' election,
pirouette outweigh forlorn? Seeming's
double daily, Christ to pay, the hist'ry
not the myst'ry weds the sty.

PRECISELY AND MOREOVER

I died in chance abandon, made the clearing
tough to take, or went to meet a bleat of
feigning belly crates, to fly by number to
render coil. By bait the trough is
ridden, hung tanks upon a top of
toil, or tender mute the silent, shrill
the shorn, and bear a coal to castle's
glare. Less 'parent than 'prehended
shakes time to bugger oil (the bellicosity out
(of). Sponge season, or fretful tongs with
claws.

RIDDLE OF THE FAT FACED MAN

None guards the moor where stands
Receipt of scorn, doting on doddered
Mill as fool compose compare, come
Fair padre to your pleated score
Mind the ducks but not the door
Autumnal blooms have made us snore

GETTING WISE TO THE WHEREFORES

Vexatious visage begins blunt

showcase, lacks a

plumage to sputter

inconspicuously sorrowful teeters with

neopolitan origin

go way to

oily nosebleeds, kicking

as belting

aluminum airway

(tends been slow)

to rosebud between

enabling flick, so

sallow to behave

as if extra signage

promotes *pommes frites*, impolitic

perusal of interior visualizations of

cascading hollows. Clue pinpoints

pajamas, exclusively for the

sidereal passion to remand a

balanced barometric mensch—

warmer. Swaddle as may, canned

or can not or cantankerously
loose toothed, with
crabbed blanket and an hysterical
ectopic cacorhythmia—bluesy
blouse, blustery letdown somnolence.
Hushly hailing marginal sailing. Meaning
have you aired the veils, festooned
the ——. Infelicitously carnal, suckers
for the apron's nipple, hulled
into.

SITES OF INVOLVEMENT

Stumbled and stored, this wakefulness
speaks only of decor, decoyed
by dumbfounded doors, pierce
as likely as before—all
moors. A gnat who clamps
upon this hose, in dignified
despair—abler spout to
what cannot be spare. Silence
as the breath announced spends
volumes to rescind, just
wind.

NINA'S PARTY AT JUDY'S GYM

Funny how these days lounge and flit
past seeming rancor to the fits
of fulsome plan. I have for long
endured a passion subsumed by all I
see, yet the weaving thins the layer
and the fluted hopes evaporate
in steam. Nobody launches
except to sail, but lips grow
sedulous, fingers fumble. How
little to show before a firing squad
of one's own device takes aim, replies.
Conversation, not communion, communities,
makes this world glow—lit
but not consumed.

EPIPHANIES OF SUPPRESSION (3)

No, it's

this world

we know

little of

kindly it

hides and

gratefully we

are hidden.

So, mentality

drives the

spoon, noting

lisps' aspirant

deference. Got

to get

by without

a ladder's

seem(l)y plaque.

Where to

spin?—the

cotton lurches

for its

gin, but

fear never

trusts *its*

maker. Eyes

hold glances

to know

containedness, ignite

each store

to dissimulate

apparatus' reliquary.

Or holes

to holler

to.

HOW TO DISAPPEAR

I don't know much about art, but
I know what I don't like. Hat
packed, ready to go. As years embalm
decay, mist on wing, wits
on other. For sight is such
a short-lived fling, of bone and spewn
like tile atop the toil, who brings
Jersey-suited ploys, or what by
sought is summed, fazed onto, dub-
doused flight, charred rescinds. The suitor
blows a finer measure, capped as
pierces against alarm, which fraught
with force retards display.

SALTMINES REGAINED

Where goes the paraposturous
brain-dead morning as
cleavage relieves its
apostate narcissism?
Or hinges shingles
lipped up at
callback stations, entering
and then cordoning
off of delinquent
(or is it derelict?)
fiberboard. Fire brands
the stake, disbands the
song, as if twirls
might array, pearls
might prolong. Seek
having sucked
& sucker calls
that seer these
plots, wading to
allure & spun
into glass.

ROWING WITH ONE OAR

So the sieve is sifted, the spun attended to
A token of foreign charm, lost here among
The can of category, disdain of
Destination. You catch if only to amount
As cord-draped prongs befit of all
But tides are guided, a needle through
The Hey, or what's about faces, our
Armenian friend who hopes to
Cure his ponies and put away the
Rest as hedge 'gainst eschatology
Or moral 'dolotry. Planes down
The view the better to begin to
Build it up. Snow bound or wind
Chapel. *Here* becomes the premised
Glare—bowling and then bowled
Over.

TARGETS OF OPPORTUNITY

We share these sediments, sentiments
out of hope of passing through
divides into an uncrossed
wildness that never can
arrive, that always already
has been sold. The world
inhabited by its core
of molten planes of
pain—the loss which
binds the gap, to
break against such
lore as those our father's
father's father told to tune
the flood of
days.

WHOSE LANGUAGE

Who's on first? The dust descends as
the skylight caves in. The door
closes on a dream of default and
denunciation (go get those piazzas),
hankering after frozen (prose) ambiance
(ambivalence). Doors to fall in, bells
to dust, nuances to circumscribe.
Only the real is real: the little
girl who cries out "Baby! Baby!"
but forgets to look in the mirror
—of a . . . It doesn't really
matter whose, only the appointment
of a skewed and derelict parade.
My face turns to glass, at last.

VERDI AND POSTMODERNISM

She walks in beauty like the swans
that on a summer day do swarm
& crawls as deftly as a spoon
& spills & sprawls & booms.

These moments make a monument
then fall upon a broken calm
they fly into more quenchless rages
than Louis Quatorze or Napoleon.

If I could make one wish I might
overturn a state, destroy a kite
but with no wishes still I gripe
complaint's a Godly-given right.

ROUGH TRADES

"By now I was tense, on edge, what they
were saying didn't have any meaning for
me—just some cut-rate jive in
social workers' phraseology that proved
a certain intellectualism, I supposed. But
I didn't have to listen to it; I was
going to get the hell out."

—Chester Himes, *If He Hollers **Let Him Go***

BEING A STATEMENT ON POETICS FOR THE NEW POETICS COLLOQUIUM OF THE KOOTENAY SCHOOL OF WRITING, VANCOUVER, BRITISH COLUMBIA, AUGUST 1985

I've never been one for intellectualizing. Too much
talk, never enough action. Hiding behind the halls of theories
writ to obligate, bedazzle, and torment, it is rather
for us to tantalize with the promise, however false, of speedy
access and explanatory compensation. *A poem should not
be but become.* And those who so disgrace their
pennants, however and whomever so deafened, shall tar
in the fires of riotous inspiration and bare the
mark of infancy on their all too collectivist breasts. Terrorism
in the defense of free enterprise is no vice; violence
in the pursuit of justice is no virgin. This is
what distinguishes American and Canadian verse—a topic
we can ill afford to gloss over at this
crucial juncture in our binational course. I
did not steal the pears. Indeed, the problem
is not the bathwater but the baby. I want
a poem as real as an Orange Julius. But
let us put aside rhetoric and speak as from one
heart to another words that will soothe
and illuminate. It is no longer 1978, nor for
that matter 1982. The new fades like the shine
on your brown wingtip shoes: should you simply
buff or put down a coat of polish first? Maybe the shoes
themselves need to be replaced. *The shoes themselves:* this is the
inscrutable object of our project. Surely everything
that occurs in time is a document of that

time. Rev. Brown brings this point home when he
relates the discomfort of some of his congregation
that formulations of a half- or quarter-, much less
full-decade ago are no longer current to today's
situation. The present is always insatiable because
it never exists. On the other hand, the past
is always outmoded and the future elides. Light
travels slowly for the inpatient humanoid.
Half the world thinks the night will never end
while another half sweats under the yoke of unrelenting
brightness. It's time to take our hats off
and settle in. The kettle's on the stovetop, the
centuries are stacked, like books, upon the shelf.
Bunt, then buzz.

READING THE TREE: 1

A litter bin vexes the mill, we howl
for more. The complex call, the xenophobic
alternatives, with related concerns having
reached a critical mast. What is shared, at
best, is intriguing, your life, this
surrogate social struggle. Language a
sorrow gate, malled environ, woody
ardour. In doing so clearly foreground,
is now plain, of particulate importance, if
only in reflected convenience. "I hate
speech" & speech don't like me none too good
either. Instead of rat brains I ate gnat
wings. East of paradise, north of the
corridor, to which none is subject, all
member. Stepping through the water to the
mops. Snow covers the boats, smothers
the folks. Otherwise, the damage already
glows, slows, mows. A cause, a
pose, something on vapor (they used to be
the leaders of the avant garde, but now
they just want to be understood). *Only
fragments are (f)actual.* Shapes sloshing,
the wave of pandemonium or gloss of
consternation, mute in the (a) sea that only
scatters. Everyone keeps shouting
in my ears: but rest assured, dear papa,
that these are my very own sentiments and
have not been borrowed from anyone. I want
to put *this* word *here* (the dead

should have known better). Folding cups
to receive syllables. The
flimsy charms, hysteric prognostication. She looked
so nice you kind of wonder about her
husband. O soredea! O weedsea! Men in
Aida are appealing, aren't they? A day
with Achilles in silly garb, Apollo on a
deep hill—all pay high prices for full
head, misunderstood as a measure
of distance across a level field of things
each defining a spiral dressed in shadow,
tracing the rustling of language's identity
turned into creamed figures, like constant
commotion, repeatedly connoting. *This*
I saw and said before dis-
covering the wren. An ordinary, empty
tune, inflated yet miniature, elbowed
enzymatically. Stillness
crumpling; holding the map that is
unattached, figurative boot in backstage
foolscap. Apply thumb
for answer: insatiable
fatigue. For polis is peals,
pelts, pages. Deep snow
behind a red temple. Last week I
wrote, "This morning
the swelling's died & pilots
compete for the sober hue in a pile
of broken-up sentiments (tenements)." *Not
fixed!? When then!?* All that
aside, a girl is running. (—Don't

tell *me* a girl is running.)
Wild vistas inside blistering
paint (pant, pummel the
chimera). My vision of aspects
houses prefabrication (the enigma
rose before the triangulated
nose). (Looking on hopelessly
like children eating baloney.)
Derision thrives whether or not
it is possible to reply. I have
destroyed my ammunition to make way
for an ocean that shadows me as
I walk in the unpaid-for park, yet
the traffic draws away from me and I
am ill at ease listening to the sugar
pour and the gravity steam. Shall
we stroll into focus or submerge
in ponds: example is gratified
by its spout. On the way to L.A. I
meet a surrogate for you in a bar, give him
room in the passenger seat and desultory
conversation, a smoke, kisses, blowjob,
encouragement, $5, concerned disturbed
uptight look. How can I characterize you
that way? You're really gone. I confuse
you with the reader. I can't scream
in space. I come at myself (I'm
not interested in *pursuing* lines
of thought): you can hear the shapes
and grates of the swoon. If to witness,
if to judge, which is to say exacerbate

the only sign of mottled hiss, embroidered
embrasure. These
are not my words but those that summer
gives me, with a tenderness quite
unknown in the real world, where
there is little to remember but
stormy days. I would have a house
of my own, with a bay of pastel
miasma, reality leaking
from its edges, as the context
conditions. Therefore, my style
seems to have fallen to
pieces, deteriorated
in the three-year interim
between books; others
may write better-made poems
but those poems with their elegant
turns of phrase, their vivid
imagery, even their conceptual
excellence, often add up to nothing.
Either poetry is real as, or realer than,
life, or it is nothing, a stupid
& stupefying occupation for zombies.
For my poetry is informed by
something inside that doesn't
flinch & won't budge. & I
could never have done it alone.
I may work in the factory but I glide
to the music of the anemones.

READING THE TREE: 2

The part plots a spindle but the
true scales wattle off the clock.
At at which pops as someone
nodules quarts, wholly non-check
slowdown. Bend nothing & nothing
will bend you, jam the gorge
astride the loom, black-away to
tending send. A single everything
points: the mud of bulk, tonal
belief, perfect compassion. &
graciously pissed (oh Hannah!):
acting like a typical male
chauvinist pigsty. Nothing
comes quickly, too nervous,
bulb which whose, you thought,
screened bottom (I likes my
repeated stupid) across (don't
complete) sent(i)ence. That's all
a silhouette for obedience, the
oilcloth cuffs quip, maybe
accuses the whole world of his
darkness. You seem unable to
understand that (pygmy whitemeat):
drooping as texture, each embody
dynamite *bluntesse*, puffing
lint wheels syllabary to
tea cakes. OK? Monotonous
agitations thrown across spent
bonbons. Well well well well.

You have to enforce digestion.
May I slip through the greased
palms of sociology tonight? Without
even knowing what it *looks*
like. I'm always resistant, while she
sets as the shadow of my
thoughts. Passion toys curiously: seem
to recall, holding what you expected
to be left out, finalized
occurrence, past eventual
pronouncing. At home, it means
light to them. Luck as forced
movement, passionate bondage.
Only by the moon's house, the
light's frost . . . Arm
jammed, meaning's glance coats
cool, cones emblem's jars, erupts
immense drone, cucumbered out
of clock, load dickering. Tuned
full, leveraged gline. This
is the evening before I ask,
my hands hardened to let water
in, or substance, acceleration,
a line of sight inflating to
become extinct. *Listen
to reason.* It's only a few hours
away and plunges down. Great
logs of the moon: The things that
make up daily life, meteorites and
meteroids, air, food, housing.
Years stars caught in space.

My reefs, my trees having fallen.
Then the reader crowds the page
with the rush of ideas: a portable
altar strapped to his back, waving
fables and faces and manoeuvering
between points, holes in clouds,
condensing into a stream of ink.
The present moss tears backward
shading the grief
of heaven's earthlessness, and melting
into empty air. Blind love for the
future, I used to say, as if
measure met my grave. Dreams
wheel their pale course, we write
in sand. . . . But you've
changed—money, self-destruction,
metabolism, large major things,
the real stuff. I remember you
in certain immense situations: how
the timing was wrong, or don't
surge with me now, how what I
could accept purples your words,
flash images of fractional chance,
crystal methodology, giddy
visibility. When she smiles
another star is lit; when she laughs,
she drops the balloon. Carrying
swollen changes that rip in the whirl
responsiveness makes. Lining
the pictures & deliriously
swinging upward toward our hats.

I used to be American but now I just
speak English. Conventicles sledging
tumbled delusions, danishes in
the pool. As per permanent noncling 100%
banlon fodder (semidistinguishable
dent) nods out to liquidating
dropsy (would like to shut him out
of misbegotten congelation of
debasements). I mean I wanted to hear
everything, not any way to pass
judgment, as if one could remain
or could stand aside from things we
saw. Light long enough to recover,
to gain a second beam. Mother tongue,
father pastrami. Then one evening I
twist myself around, keeping track
of all my loose ends, which I hadn't
expected because I'd always come out
as component parts, so I cut back, can't
see, at which point I'm facing
perhaps the ablative absolute,
humiliation of a class system to
create final segment but now stands
by itself, in someone else's
clothes, as a way to set off to just
where I've wanted to be all along:
spectacularly encumbered but
composed (some might say extended), a
surface you can't hide in front of,
or out of fumbling exhalation—tense
windows—sound a press, gap a spill.

Browsing for ice, the fragrance of
its labor staggers outside the house
of Rimes, green bottles smoked as
they're hitched, the fish in the
pail, and the pail in my hand. Later
we go to lunch, but now we talk shoes.
I began all this in April, 1972, at
3:35 am. Those were the intentions
I wrote down. In this way, from
the outside, I put everything in.
On April 11 I dreamt the history
of all people in the world, good &
evil. In June I started it again
& what started it was that I wrote
this: Her pins prick my skin.
A blinding wedge, maybe the shape
of selection (seduction): you leave
traces impossible to tear, I want
to get out of here. *Hide me.*
White verges, whirrings of remorse,
seep through the terminal, a kind of
restored diligence, radial in its
appetite, when the evening shuts in
space or relaxes its axes
in translucent thirst, ineluctably
tainted by tendency. Whose blousing
anecdotes within which trenchant
anarchies tour ardor, penchant for
flatulent latitudes backing into
breath. The impact of the pipe
like ice cream at the end of a

sequence of themes memorialized
in a pinhole. Blurry wheezes in the
ricochet, crushing puffs of
swelling fellowship. The Hudson
lies, we get over who dies. Plethora
jellies where the Persian Gulf
empties into the roof. Say it,
damn it! Then suddenly, a sedan
comes around blasting and I drop
to the sidewalk behind a hydrant, squinting
to get the plate number. (Impotence
itself should not discredit a man,
but no one considers supporting it.)
It is seven o'clock. I put on my
coat and hat. Samples are recorded
with a spinning arc, balancing
incontinently to find the proscenium.
Yet politics excited them, the avarice
for neglected ideas under the locks
in the hallway. No end
in sight—nothing breaks, or
spend all the time pending, sense
of where, whose to what's, seen
as sidereal blink, as in: sure could use
a cold drink, a hot potato, an
exact definition (remonstration). I'm
afraid because I know a word
without having seen it or read it.
(All experience is conditioned by expectation.)
& my feelings yearn for names known
only by interval and tone. The points

connect *only once*. I come
to the door, I stop at the door, I
push the door open.

"Reading the Tree: 1 and 2" have as their source the poems collected in In the American Tree, *edited by Ron Silliman (Orono, Maine: National Poetry Foundation, 1986).*

OF TIME AND THE LINE

George Burns likes to insist that he always
takes the straight lines; the cigar in his mouth
is a way of leaving space between the
lines for a laugh. He weaves lines together
by means of a picaresque narrative;
not so Hennie Youngman, whose lines are strict-
ly paratactic. My father pushed a
line of ladies' dresses—not down the street
in a pushcart but upstairs in a fact'ry
office. My mother has been more concerned
with her hemline. Chairman Mao put forward
Maoist lines, but that's been abandoned (most-
ly) for the East-West line of malarkey
so popular in these parts. The prestige
of the iambic line has recently
suffered decline, since it's no longer so
clear who "I" am, much less who *you* are. When
making a line, better be double sure
what you're lining in & what you're lining
out & which side of the line you're on; the
world is made up so (Adam didn't so much
name as delineate). Every poem's got
a prosodic lining, some of which will
unzip for summer wear. The lines of an
imaginary are inscribed on the
social flesh by the knifepoint of history.
Nowadays, you can often spot a work
of poetry by whether it's in lines
or no; if it's in prose, there's a good chance

it's a poem. While there is no lesson in
the line more useful than that of the picket line, the line that has caused the most adversity is the bloodline. In Russia
everyone is worried about long lines;
back in the USA, it's strictly souplines. "Take a chisel to write," but for an
actor a line's got to be cued. Or, as
they say in math, it takes two lines to make
an angle but only one lime to make
a Margarita.

WAIT

This is the way to start a sentence about startling a sentence. Here is the tense that has not heart, that tramples beyond its own infirmity. O! how exquisite is the loss of all that we have shared, all that we might better have hoped only to have lived for. Pleased, said I, who cares so little about such things, who'd rather be a mast on a plumb of piddle than underlit by dunks . . .

At this point dive into second. Soon I will try to correct a foil trivial to all but those who see behind a wet-pressed fin. Or would this mean that all was tossed in this here twirl? What am I to do sayeth the elderly man. I will goes into these houses that you have made for me and will tell you all I slate.

So it crawls off far into the sky that never answers
Where daylight falls but knows neither you or ye
        Fall into my arms of twilight
          As I kiss the pit that stomachs not its pith
And in this return to faithful sentience, gaze but have not
Fear for all I try will bring to nought this pail of peers.

To say again.
To say it here/
Only this
can I know, that where I fly together will you warp that
abode embrace my flight.
    Or shall it only be that here do swim upon the grace of all
that has o'ercome this vault of

    sceptres. Steeped in vain revamp
or put upon
        at reason's heap.

    Not to say or not to
    As

with this gaze upon failed Mystery
or in the giving go, the living loss
strikes against these bows

Which only says to this that will go variously to bay for noisesome
        sleep.
                          Stern

among the frolicsome pompadors.

HOUSE OF FORMALDEHYDE

It's not where you're going, it's
Where you've been. Dateline
In the harbor. Fellow rushes
For funding, fuming, flipping
Flaccid: rimless erosion, witless
Emulsification. As on a bent,
Meal, plaid, plane, a girl
Holds a pail, defends a swirl

Stumbling for eviscerated lead hooks
Englotted, Nordic stoops
Whosover irradiates decay, plunged
As pediment, foaming sail, lining the
Shifts with spongy (spectacular) spatulas.

Horatio of spell-bent positioning, fusing
Co-spaniel foresight and copper-wire calumny
Against the grain of saddlestitch cornmash.
Precisely giddy, morosely fecundated. Snorkling
& then snookered. Roadside rest-test adjoined
To defamilial tireiron. (Unhooks what's
Best left loose.) As was fonder than
Revenants. Neither a fender nor a succotash
Be. (Merely a spittoon of her petunia.) Seeking
Not or seeing blotted—wave-high the croon,
Defrock the peeling Argonaut. I would
Not sink her ship nor span her
Border as lacking sun-stained
Catapults. Neither have I . . .

Whose deflection can only pronounce insipience
As the promise leadens enactment
& the dusted gables parrot the stick to which
Only lessening accounts. The serpentine miles
Of the long-laundered parade dissolve
In gulps, becalmed forays. Having hidden
My amulets & fired my token,
Alone on a dust-dark sea, with only
Thee. Or wails oasis, deeded ground
Where foot cannot fall, & felled, retains.

WEATHER PERMITTING

She hits the
lake and now
it's time for
      Like
five'll get
one, ten'll get/
roaring into the
blast of last
year's rasp,
or bereft on a
beach outside
a full-scale
rivet. "We've
got the best
employee
incentive plan
around: they don't
work
out, we
fire
them." Slipping

in the freeze-
dried morning,
sipping on old
trends turned
sour, new
friends turned
the corner
to a bitterer break
than cast
iron. Bust
your pajamas
'cause the
calendar is
dormer. Hail as
the whittle in a
grain of plow.

FORCE OF FEELING

Nothing is absurd when people are being killed
around you like flies. Some way out
of the mire, denuded dust. Checking
(chalking) as it turns—spin of
latched delegation, which forecasts
felicitation. Not yet to dance, to tip
as tone delays, ensnares. Silly widget
creatured by antebellum forest rangers
as if or when, who without wanting withers.
Meanwhile, at glance disposed
to any glaze while splay is act, foremost
foremast incised by the veridical coat
check boy swore he never took no
cookery. Swell, just as well really, better,
just forget it, forget it was ever
mentioned.

THE PURITAN ETHIC AND THE SPIRIT OF CAPITALIZATION

                                                                     constancy—or, rather

          questions about

              notably, mark

        at which the

                locus

            which this

                    put

    not all. If

                what once

enables

          "cold fish"

  of the severe

                          image is uniform

       a steady. Ministers

            thus

      perceive—and in fact

  simply will

by looking

            nor to whether

      objects? In my

                        employ

  opposed the oscillating

for example, the ringing of bells
                              Behavior in the streets
         someone bumps
                    with an even temperament
         moves abruptly
                                   (petty quarrels
         strenuously unleashed
         clutter (well for
                              mood about on self
              extend simultaneously
    can be illusioned
                              in both rude &
         showering insipience
                              Help to ought
              it be of manners
    Quota
                                   have ployed
              "infirmary"
                                        over something
                                   (view, with
                    bottom all broked out
         endorsing a
              plausal relent
    this par &

FILED REPORT

There is no sign other
than the sigh of this
unveiled removal.
Given the mixed
abjures, the journey
no longer appeases.
No easy answer
abides, yet laxness
is taken as virtue
& bands of
discontent are
disconnected. One
aimlessly distorts
as play for 'plause
(not that silence
cures). Torrents
of overcompensation
showboat guest-laddered
dipsomania.

In it but *out of* it
("I need a drink").
*Nail down your
battens.* Impressed into
service, substitution for
(sure pest).
Substitution blocked.

Or promise more
than hope could
hope more than
promises.
Angry without spears,
or rigged to buoy-blind try
against detour.

Bigelow or whigged out.

Be a blooper! (Can't
get a hard-on
with the light
on.)

"It's like having
our own baby. It's
so cute & cuddly.
It's better than
yours
because we're puppets
too."

Marshalling all my resources to play the
role of a writer—a singular act of
concentration to put out all that would
distract me from this assignment, all
that would discredit my performance.

Falling back into
quasi-overt reverse
psychobabble, patently
trumpeted
bounces
up & off.

Chewing gum
&
spitting
at the same time.

Better to bark
out of fear than
fear to bark—

THE POET FROM ANOTHER PLANET

So they drove
& the night
becoming day became

a knife numb
and gray &
the all-toothed

allocation climbed into
the realm of
the beautiful and

lime. Thus aimless
it becomes painless
the genetic substrate

that courses remorses
and bids goodbye
to the anonymous

dispersion. A general
economy as if
to pray that

half a loaf
would be not
so good as

no loaf (half
a boast not
so good as

no boast). Restive
without rest, anxious
without anxiety. So

many fears, none
real. There's a
vision but there'll

never be a
visitation.

FOAM POST

Lose track of where seven Moabite
Everything the stove as agent you
Devolved and basically are
Spunk in a minute reprobated
Adverse elemental approbation gelatinous
Curio sung to deeds socked with
Ginger and gold sullen and then
Surrendered by cave-lit trestle
Of simpering slug-down egress.
Or parts of guarantee cleaned
Out pockets an unclasped shake
Rant about owing restricted
Tributary and wakes on
These stupid tires implements
Trashed in an overgrown bestiary
In a vest of tiers. Notable
Inclination: "Too much belly an' no'
Eno' brain." Sermons of
Vibration who'll holler before
Discrepancy tuck jug—
Tinsel of titularly vague versions
Verging behind programmable dual
Dipsticks. Everything seen so far
Away and more produce on other
Seismographic orifice bundle branching
Toxemia inadmissible as to stuck-up
Steam stadium circuits bored cauldron.
Neptune's climb from the ducks to the
Decks (oilcloth) solvent to dementia

Spud repertory condominium. Flown
Boast (Kelly-green incapacitator): which
Is very natural ("I do not care for the part about
Pirates"), sometime aquatic ("Solange had to say
It was over a long time before"), unconscionably
Pede-like ("the soldiers marched valiantly
To their reward") and preternaturally triumphant
("Available evidence suggests a lack of
Further routes of inquiry"). Periodicity
Or piquant insolvency (not currency but the
Fear of is the). Rain rain
Raining inside my tailored suit. "Twelve
Yards, only twelve yards over, at the
Intersection of Vein and Vine—another
Lawn being mowed! Another
Gracious day!" Not to have to
Not to say, not to have to have
To, not to have to prey, not to
Have to, not to have to feel
Not to, not to have to have to
Say. Pink lemons on the orange
Lime tree.

RIOT AT 111 STATION

If I lose my temper you're totalled.
Sallow trays of disgenerate plush, flushing
the balcony of derision, conviction's
tumor. Lost my glasses
flashes. As might
incense a prod, wherever it
clogs. Suddenly
distends into arced, incoordinate
future frisson.
Mongrel angle detoured, brulant
and trampled, of volutuality manque
"as nauseous and tedious as adultery in literature".
The brick that broke the camel's sap. Fit to be
frenzied (funny you don't look
tumescent). Fat Boy's famous
Jew-Punching Contest ("NO
CREDIT REJECTS HERE").
As benefits bereavement
in whom return might anchor.

SEVEN FOR AOTEAROA

> Don't take
> the steak
> I ain't
> Dunedin.
> —Robert Creeley, *Hello*

Ear Shot

Here is the spare

aside the locker room

where I am marooned

Thermal Gardens

This

is not the blue

lake or pink

lake or orange

lake—just a

lake, landed

by an unobliging

perseverance who

snaps, world

weary, not worried

& all the

pushchairs plod

along the potted

parts.

The Beauty of Brevity, the Bananas of Antibes

Poussin did not eat baloney.

Harsh Light

I don't think I

can keep her

from the lighter

much longer

Free Turn

If I had a dime
for every hour I've had
peace of mind
I'd still be a poor man

[or]

I was gay & carefree
but now I am grave with
responsibility

No Pastrami

Walt! I'm with you in Sydney
Where the echoes of Mamaroneck howl
Down the outback's pixilating corridors

Historic Bookplates of California

No end to envy.

SLOWED REASON

Poetry is sediment

I wipe off the windshield

The mindshield, a process

Of such and such refrain

An original instance

Of many waiting

The field of shifting

Expenses reclaim the years

Remainders of what is there

A battle of listening

Degree of fuming

Autopsies the barometer

In children's voices, taut or piercing

Moments, leers, discharge

Against a flattened calculus of indication

(I can tell by the feeling)

Reminders to explain

Insane parts of an entire flesh

A map, a sword, a monkey.

Moisture of talk, minimizes mimicry

Mummy's condensation, a repetitious scrawl

Of transitions from previous notes

Corresponding to functions

Parts of a closed ambition

The original instance of many

Waiting

I can tell by that

Or

"Keep your clothes on"

Process of sifting

The entire field

A calculated function of

Degree (debris)

Without which I must

Rattle a gourd filled with pieces of my own flesh

Matrices that correspond

Inverted sentiment

                    —Nick Piombino & Charles Bernstein

BEYOND THE VALLEY OF THE SOPHIST

You don't get the sense
he has a lot to say; but he says it
very well. The search
which is a deference to the caving
walls of essential acts, potential facts. Circling
caustics in seas of suits. [I]
want a phone, a sea, a
curb; body parts impede essence. (Relation

Precedes production.) Athwart
knack (flagon). As homemade
bestiary enthrottles boheme. *Bruce
is bruised by bluster* (Buster). Fight
fire with water (warper). "This
is a powerful, original, and deeply
moving work and many will
find it a disturbing one."

When in falcon time and of a ripe
rage, I bloat a board, as ever
has accord in a day-long waft . . .
as or like may gird, sift, stultify,
perish, churl. Anyone blessed with
pumice. He said he had a mouse
in his hard disk. Then apoplectic, disappointed.

"I purely couldn't tell you, partly
couldn't consider, penultimately
unavoid[avail]able." Even Pope John Paul II

agrees. "I have read Professor Bell's
letter with amazement. In my review I said
his research was fascinating and most skillfully
presented. As for
the misgivings I felt (and still

Feel), they were expressed in as considered a
manner . . ." Those things
which I beheld as child—chair, table
floor—concrete, that meant a life. Or
blind to purloined recall, dodges for
bull or Bill, only to inappropriately
will. These china dolls, Moroccan
scrawls: the cost of it all.

Retention that squanders its own demand,
see-sawing and then fawning. "My ink
is not good, my paper dirty, & I
am altogether ashamed." Standing,
stunned; strutting, stunted. He
who is lost hesitates and hesitating finds
(but not what he looked for). She
who meditates is tossed. Let geese

Be geese! (He does not care whose house he
sets on fire as long as he can warm himself
by the blaze.) There stands the hood,
there the barking knife. *Take a scissors
to write.* "She sure put a spook
in my wheels!" Like two dogs with one
prick. Nor cast your hose before
gnomes; that is, skin them but don't

Fleece them. For it's better to be led
by the nose than by the hairs, better
to be led by the nose than to have a lead
nose. Which is to say, he was
a hatchet without a handle, a pudding
in a puddle. What a muddle!
"I only say suppose this supposition," propose
this proposition. Not a tragedy, just an

Inconvenience. & don't be harsh without
a reason. (Just after she screams
she picks up her bottle & dreams.)
Then we came upon a grand beech forest
Where once I lost my good friend Morris.
Willingly, I'll say I've had enough. Wet
as a mule and twice as
disgusted. Take my husband,

Please! But the pleasures are entrusted
to the wrong partitions: the cant of
intellectual fashion (Paris) lies
a decade behind leather design (Milano). Harsh,
that is, without accuracy. For with Rehnquist
& Meese, the only ones with rights
are the unborn and the police. & reigning over all,
the Great Communicator—master of deceit. No release.

Heave, hoe this
firmament.
What is here
only that; no
less. The tide
pulls back its
brim—in which
we spin.

The prolonged hippopotami of the matter
swivel for their breakfasts, fall in the middle landing soft
with the horse shrill of honeysuckle, to the decimated
   acid of the sweet
tub. They are hobbled, dejected
& lie frozen with salted humbling.
To the ocean of shorn horizon, averting America's
sentient emptiness, here where the body's sightless ascent
revolts in paltry recompense.

Obscurity beckons from down the block
oblivion, too, bids me come & knock.
The water calls me but I shall not go
for a man's place is on the sho'.
You can sing and you can pray & you can shout lots
but you'll never get to Heaven without a box.
Lox & bagels, bagels & lox, kreplach
is on the stove, time for a plate of hocks.

I'd ask that you call me by my Christian name, Buddy
(since I don't know your name, I hope you don't mind
    my calling you that).
It's not a lot to ask; purely, it's a small thing
but I think it'd help to bond the cement between us
put us on indistinct terms, if you know what I mean.
What I want to bring across to you, Buddy
is the vanity of conceits
though you may call it what you please—

The story is told that a man came to a house noted for
    its views
& was told, look to the West, at the mountain ranges that
    loom over the land
& was told, look to the South, at the turquoise-blue lake
    shimmering in the blue-bright sun
& was taken, then, to an Eastern balcony, overhanging
    a garden unrivaled in its varieties of plants & flowers
& he looked to the North, at the thick-grown forest
& listened to the birds that filled the branches of the
    cascading trees
& he was ushered to the Western windows
& he said, "But I've already seen that."

THE PERSISTENCE OF PERSISTENCE

"I find myself in a world of forces which
act upon me, and it's they, and not the logical
transformations of my thought which determine
what I shall ultimately believe."

—C. S. Peirce

FEAR OF FLIPPING

Presently, peasants are heard yodelling in the distance.
"It's the strain, two liters of Mercury and never
enough flotation devices—how many more times do
we have to ask": shards of bucolic pastry anchored
against cactus cabinets, Nantucket buckets. Sadly
to state a grew-quite-a-lot-since-last-look, nut-
flack visage advancing the caucus of Caucasians, the
too-near / too-far avoidance contraption destiny tears
(as in pears not peers) from Everyperson's buxom
brow. God, so much thought to be poisoned with and Lusty
Lucretius gone all these years (Luscious Lucretia pawned
for a prized pony ride): alack, this blighted Border, containing
sectionate moorage and amalgamated heartburn, flitters
its last edge, applauds its appalling prescience. For
a fan is the best hat, and the void mind the finest
conquistador—valiant without prostration, generous without
justice. . . . never inflicting out of fear, but not fearing
to inflict, as Uncle Hodgepodge put it. "All gored
up on dickering and hope"—familiar freight to
the returning antelope. Sinking into the quicksand that is
a life, eyes already under, legs, cries; so a subterranean
probe goads or litters with predetermined inkblots and
galvanized regrets: not to get it ripped or not
to get it rigged, surely a pain in the caverns
of illumination's erasure, vituperation's cradle.
Gone are the glaze; now all hollow to get hallow
and break the bank of promise on the shore of
presumptuous ill will. Oppress or be suppressed or
cry *hornets* in a den of bumbling bees. The walls

are our only floors and the floors, like balls, repel
all falls. Adequate to any sense of sediment, as 'garbage
heap' exchanges for so-called overall mesh, or
disappointed not to have been, as 'arbitrary' reduces to
'faker,' *wallow* to *value of*. "I love you so
much and I hate this war so much." Frames comparable
to apparently, and have dippier or ferrets
because you don't, cleats beyond periodization
patched at nod to reliance—take a walk.
Sparked just the same, doubly blackground ("I'd
like to see you waddle your way out of this
one") of an anyway able, especially wailing, no
matter how good. Does before doing, trends when
trend, inventories overload. Buzz is
the word, two on Tuesday, and then nobody
knows nothing but will cost but. Big Deal at
Contestable Parameter. Mood shift
or blurred gift. "If you don't like it
colored in, you can always xerox it and see it all
gray." Or else smuggle leers with guilt-edged
cheer. "You mean, image farm when you've got bratwurst?"
You mean you have a life outside this page? Not
on my greeting list: creation stares at null scooper. Dulled
dodge—but good to get hit *some*times. But surely the jumps
open chasms; yet the danger for the night watchman
is turning against the dark, or animating it with
demons and devouring them; and gain no sustenance. More
toward is there, added to some, is beyond and
present. Fat-bottom boats. Only fire will erase
the pain of having done or not done what was
done or not done. *Sheep sheep don't you know*

the road. Intimate essence hurtled into prepubescence
and mangled by the lurch. Behind this metaphor
lies Descartes, pulled by a train of horses. "It's
been years and twice as many tears." Only the world happens
and racing to get near enough. Cornered by. Something
snapped—"like those nasty people with attitude do."
Singing fa la la, fa fa la or doodling with a billy
club. A dab of adagio—humble and then humped.
"A sideshow freak suffers from fits of uncontrollable
laughter that prove to be fatal." While according to Jones,
Freud was fed at the breast, as one would expect. "Hands
that have touched ham will never touch mine" (can't
see the forest for the wheeze). Half
breed, half burrow. Or linked with
steam of pink: never the big
man or boy or bison, only the tongue-
tied tightrope stalker, witness
and then witless. Bounce back or bounce
by, the husks are salted and the fruit
is dry. Yet there will always be a there
whether here or ne'er. As opposed to
will include bending, funny to see, title
is (in the sense of bells) perfectly eliminated
demitasse or more inclusions, three-camp
world-weary, crazed by mostly had makes, pull
to find out the plug. Here's the stage—
wasn't any of them toys? Felt very poured, humming
and "stepped into," not being as part of. Hook
in second thoughts, choices like thematic
trousers splitting perception in boomeranging tutelage. What troubles
is troubling—not dealing with disagreement as

disagreement but turning it into a test
of scholarship or morality. The fact is
none of these kinks are going to see red. Was
to construct a thin skin, in every
major way, take it like this, expose it and deflate
it. In an angry mood, why assume a realer
hidden truth comes out? Somehow when something—
you leap, is said would rather ("offensively
sloppy and ill-informed"). If I have reservations
they pale before the list of villainies you offer.
Time and tiredness, to coin a phase. *Heaven's
gate is nickel plate* (shook up and blistered). It's
very hard to invoke just how immaculate such reception
would have to be. & the volcano roared &
the people said this is a message but there was none
to say what it meant & the people wept that
they might understand & the lava flowed. Waxy
figures in an airbrushed memory of moderate
times and tinkling moral sensations—the chassis
with no suspension, the heart without its
pump. Blue sky that absorbs such feats
as these or those, caring not, nor
staring, immutable redresser of,
and the fallow heather that once was
treasured. Going not, then
gone. Lips like lisps—
sibilant and sweet. Or
vie for vision on a deck
of pearl—hugely inchoate
brick mixed with spit
and darn-near squawks.

For material is the in-
substantial stuff that is craved
in sprawl of
gravures—arrangements of another
day, cyclic hay. Where
beauty is not found for
want of good or bad
and echoes carry ingots
themself to turn upon
gradient's unmitigating fold.
A cart that hauls in grandeur
grim resemblance of resplendent
tongues—swerving spigot of an
unappointed dome.

POCKETS OF LIME

Everything has happened, nothing
        possessed. The lawn engages
Its constituent appraisers. Burrows
        fold by, unaccosted by memories of
Synergies the doorjamb clops
        to. Boulevards
Beam in the near distance while
        on its wand the
Hermits are organizing affinity
        clusters. In the cab, desiccated Dominicans
Cop to outtakes from "Take the 'A' Train" as
        the band plays late
Into a night that never comes. On deck,
        a shipboard romance turns
Sordid when the expiration date embossed
        on a Ouija board is
Overlooked. The days so blinding, before
        you know it's time
For another frame of Limbo at
        Club Lumbago. "There's no
Buggy like the Buggy that ate my
        baby in the summer of '82." Not
Two days left, scouting under the eaves
        for thrown-away cheese &
Mink fleas. One chord crests, no
        place for more, when
You 'ear 'er, down by the Walla Walla
        Feedway. (As if foreign or foreign-
Scented.) Nothing has happened, everybody

has been processed. The
Elevator leads to a flight of bronzed
   stairs that ends near a
Picture of your majestic presentiment,
   rather noisier than had
Been or would be anticipated or
   asphyxiated, in some ways a
Damp cloth and light dusting would have
   done as well. *At this point*, the
Nasobiliary tube is inadvertently
   dislodged; before replacing it, we
Decide to insert an endoprosthesis. "Worms
   in brain, worms in
Stomach, how'm gonna worm me way
   out o' here." You see, you are
What you tear, but only the baker knows
   what the bread's been fed. "But the big
Question, which they don't discuss, is
   what kind of glue the man was
Using." A soul as soft as Detroit, a
   bile as big as a bagel—though the
World's not made of muslin and the only
   cosmic gas is static
Electricity. *How would you treat the patient
   now?* Would you leave the
Tubes in place for continuous drainage? Refer
   for laparotomy? Or
Perform balloon dilation of the stricture
   and endoscopic sphincterotomy?
Keep in mind that the bilirubin is down to
   1.6 mg/dl and the platelet count

Remains low at 4,000. Where the harp is
        the loneliest fire station, adorned
With piecemeal crescendi and unaugmentable
        nosegay, enlisted into an action
Encumbered by touch, hostage to
        decision: derision's ubiquitous
Breatholizer, haphazard and blousy.
        Double space everything; use *soft* not
Hard returns; use
        word wraparound
If available; spike headings, don't
        center anything; set tabs
For tabulars instead of spacing over or
        among or inside or in between or across or
On top of or throughout or beside or in place
        of; provide extra space between
Text and other Elements; use letters for
        numbers where possible, numbers for
Letters as necessary; order pages
        consanguineously (don't start
Numbering from one). You may be asked to
        type simple "genetic codes" in the process;
These serve as placeholders; do not
        type such codes without specific instruction
From the Instruction Terminator.
        Everything has progressed, nothing
Has occurred. The firetruck roars
        to the Lake District while at the encampment
All that's left are
        flesh wounds. THE DAY THE $
STOOPED. BILLIONS FOR BROWNIES. BABY'S FIRST

                    BATH. DESIGNATED VICTIM. "There's
No question that he's got a big Freudian
                    thing." "Arguably the most argumentative
Poet in America." "You need to know that when you
                    infringe on somebody else's
Profitability, you have to have a clean
                    operation or a load of
Protection." "We're
                    going through this coffee like
A fly through butter." Keep in mind, however,
                    that many of these changes need not
Cost a leg nor require you to overhaul your
                    imaginary. Clean, uncluttered shelves,
For instance, do not require a wrecking
                    crew. Neither do neat, legible, complete,
manuscripts. Similarly, you may not have been
                    born with attributes of a Greek
God nor the fashion sense of a Milan
                    model, but you know what you'd
Like to see in a competent art professional.
                    I am sure that a stained smock, seen
Through the haze of hemp smoke, is not what
                    you have in mind. We won't
Put up with that in our physician or stockbroker, then
                    why should we expect our readers
To accept less from us. "Don't question
                    my similes," said the supple senorita. "Don't
Mess with my metonymies," cried the mandarin
                    matador. (He kept his prosodic
Devices in a toolbox on the table of
                    the padded basement shelter near the

Washer-Dryer and Automatic Pump.) Not
    liberty but the leer of liberty
Lulls the laddies from their crusted
    craters, the jaded from their lard-like
Ladders.   . . . and the ladies, with their crimson
    laces, Bill and Lou, Viv and
Stu. Or saying:
    Broiled, broiled in the broiler with lemon
Or poached, poached with some water, or
    fried, fried with butter in a pan on a stove
In a kitchen. The green so green in the afternoon
    light so no longer color but a
Cavern of expectancy jelled into a reel of
    gypsies dancing a pellucid romp
On the altar of Nostradamus, vicar of the implausible
    audibles, then cast upon the foam
Of a sailor's groan. Thus, certainty confronts
    us but we cannot be sure of it—
A surrogate holding, cradled in the mist of
    an impossible necessary, and lost
To its purpose, or our own. Vagueness, in
    which belief is mute, & manifest . . .
Even one thing can make a display. And there
    was surfeit of singularities, odd
Lots of broken middles, splintered
    threads—eidetic deniers as Michael once
Put it—for to deny is measure of our
    heft; even small coins can be traded
Or stolen. *The Unquiet Journey of Martin Heidegger.*
    As in the expression, 'What clock is it?'—
"One clock," "three clock," "eight clock." For

           anything said is significant — & much that
Is not said but only spoken, hinted —
           tossed from a glazed eye to a
Nearing touch. And what the senses
           but limiting scanners, combing the
Ineffable to produce sound, searing
           the seemless to appear as
Sour? *Soaring, senseless*
           night, of no limit, that
None have known, or
           could wish to — "Pipe
Down, you pipsqueak," said the Piper, hitting
           me with a six-inch length
Of galvanized tube. In the rooms the children
           suck & blow, talking of Moholy-Nagy.
Segmenting the real: Coca-Cola franchises
           the metaphysics of
Numerosity, according 'classic' and 'new' equal
           status, the diversity of constituencies
Obliterating the elitism of "one common
           taste" of a people. (Thinking
All is secure when nothing is secure, all is
           resolved when everything is
Indissoluble.) In this sense, postmodernism coincides
           with pluralism and Daniel Bell's
Smiling. The end of idolatry is the beginning
           of commodity fetishism: God
Isn't gone away to a happier place, she's
           not napping nor hiding nor
Lying in wait, just having a snack & settin'
           back. No shit, no shoes, just

Me & my electric windmill. "But despite
		six- and seven-digit severance
Arrangements, a fall from the top can be
		grim; neither money nor the memory
Of power innoculates against frustration, greed
		or a stinging sense of injustice."
The memory of power. Do's and don't do's & could
		do's & won't do's. "My
Personal taste never enters into anything
		I do." Everything
Has been resurrected, nothing has vanished. "The regulator
		is never separated from the
Main spring." For only truth is
		reversible, lies fester
Under the skin & make it rancid. & the
		smell of lies is everywhere
& the people crave it as perfume for their
		perfume. But truth cannot be
Smelled & is as nothing & reviled as only
		nothing is—a void & a pox & an
Abomination—for what cannot be tasted nor
		heard nor smelled cannot be put to
Use & what is not abused is less than
		nothing. Busy as beagles, we
Think what we see and say what
		we gnaw. So cry not
For the beloved nor lost but for the unseen, un-
		touched that we will
Not abjure. Cry for the steam, not the machine.
		& Monsieur Madame takes me in hand
To sing the Tut-tut-aloo, yes Monsieur et Madame

           they take me in hand & sing
The Tut-tut-aloo. *Calling Ruth, Ruth*
           when there is no Ruth. Patterns
Are what we fathom, needs
           what we endure. A crack
Is not a fault nor a fall an oasis,
           neither are vases places. & I
Have known disgraces. "I wish I were
           a gurgling guppy, 'cause then I'd
Swim, yeah then I'd swim / Sure if I
           were a gulping guppy, the Atlantic
I'd spin, Pacific I'd be in." But
           you ensnare me with your wet
Cold eyes and golden ear and I ripple
           beside, bound to the tide.
Nothing has changed, everything recalls (recoils).
           The hunger of prostration, the lassitudes
Of— "I've spent half my life covering up my
           mistakes and another half trying to
Expose them." These are the ways, counting
           one and two, three and—; but
To pray is still a dance, to fray a lost
           leader . . . on the road merely
Tread, the mill seldom silenced. Everything
           is promised, everything
Delivered. Who waits waits
           in the company of women & men &
Boys, for the Messiah whose come & gone
           with no trace; for waiting is the customed
Course for those who've missed the last boat, misplaced
           the keys. No one was

Promised, no one disfigured. & the breeze
        becomes a gust but
The house does not blow down. "I can't have
        your experience, I'm not sure I
Can have my own." "Up among the curls so
        high, like a lever that's a
Sigh." The baby play with its
        fingers; this is called 'finger
Play'. Sometime it work and sometimes it
        doesn't: all the rest is
'Redolent with breathless antipathy'.
        "Where have they gone?" asked Jasper.
"To the deep dark dank & won't be back, to
        the end that has no beams."
It's your dime but it's my quarter.

BLOW-ME-DOWN ETUDE

> Ah! through the hush the looked-for
> midnight clangs!
> —William Morris, *The Earthly Paradise*

"Put her in her Chair! Put her in her
Chair!" The bleary weights of nothing-to-explain,
nobody to explain to. News of the weave, nub
of the bleep. I take what I'm given and give
what I've taken, stake what I'm bidden, dumped
when I've driven. (Upset to get.) Just when
thought, for one thing, affecting has got
to as possible point, whatever, a few
as many were and worse didn't—
but not to dwell, to fall, specifically
where was that it might, matter (formal)
given coagulation. Remember you brought,
prying to amount for, rather given your own
dizzying play in that inflection. To open up
as much of, as far as, to convey
in this respect and a sense, at the
same, more relevant in terms of revealing, finally,
forged dominions have mistook. The only
true epiphanies the ones misplaced (the
forced replacements of). Arrived with silent

fire, projector of what was faced. *We thought we might
be better than.* But the knees swell, the
feet collapses. No further shown, as if it's
only do too little, or much too much. As
if more strobe at clay could quell command: fear
frozen with fright, tautologies our
topologies; tear the midsection & loose the
rig. There was a moment that hope made
realer than the pause endured, who wept
like trawlers without recall. No villanelle to chew
nor salmon to. These tendencies arise
out of a culture and cannot be confined to those
defined them: a pound of defiance is
worth an ounce of lure. (She was a giant
of the experience of being a baby & proud
was I . . .) Summary
or tainted with coats of (jangle what
you will, where you pry—not fables with
testy, tedious tirades, waves at)
plaint. Oracular insects
infusing pseudonymous stuffed desks (stuck
decks). Rivers of lies, severs of
glides, desperate for an even chance at less
than might release, at least a vantage
to profane the holier version of these

visions, riddled with blitzkrieged
orifices, adipose titration. Moon at
worn regales; the ink its sail. Plastered
on the mesa & pacing fifty leagues
anon. *(We thought we might be better
then.)* You try to jump ahead, but fall
behind, dropped back but are conspicuously
frames. The falters make no better
flitters, along the oak and toggled plane.
Basically berserk, the body with only
organs relies upon a
peacock's prickly prudery; then
resents what will not relent. Spilt
or guided. For guilt is the burden of the whitewashed
man: for what has not been done and what cannot be
undone. "Where there is sorrow there is
holy ground." The sink cracks, the
furl falters, and Everyperson bastes its
stew. Darting and then carted; filled with
or unacquainted by. Who feeds the farmers
cornered by a row of sediment, cooled
erotics of unsublimated stokes. He
speaks but does not offer, scarcely
sweats before he swings: there is no
denouement for pebbles or for wings.

Of course, it *is* an honor to be sprinkled
out, not that it's an evanescent one: I
dislike the form and in most phases would
not see the point in, to make stab at.
That's fine, did you notice, seems an
extraordinary, if it is in, however, for
reasons that now can't see to reply
to—stupid & wildly deranged—decided
at least is a register, is having (dubious
distinction) though as you know the lack of,
loose extension, style of support, is
segmented beyond the pale. Will lessen: I
decline: one could: at least: there are:
that will: when may: though is: you
should: that might: is obvious: possibly
substantive: worthwhile bothering. The
concurrent and multiple variables affecting the flow
of the construction stream can easily . . . Loss of
pleasure in all or almost all or nearly mostly
all; unresponsive to usually pleasurable . . .
An situation amounts, the fledgling recriminations
that border on beautification: a constituency
of tissue and marrow and formaldehyde. Many
disputes involve opinions and facts
about stipulations that occurred over months

and years. Everyone does not feel well-
treated—the same slap applied with
the fine measure of meager interdiction, ignorance
of extent. For instance, your actions seem
divisive and policing of the very "community"
you desire to support. Nothing represents
anything. Billboards poster our losses. Better
jeer than leer. Waking up at least two hours
early, body movements slow or agitated, excessive
or inappropriate feelings of self-reproach.

>That's the major
>problem we always
>have in this
>
>country. We don't
>have a totalitarian
>society where we
>
>suppress the opposition.
>We have an
>information glut and
>
>we bury the
>opposition under piles
>of newsprint that

        all say the
        other thing. So
        our side gets

        to get a
        critical review in
        The Guardian, whereas

        the other side
        gets to get
        a laudatory review

        on the front
        page of the
        Times Book Review.

                                  [Michael Meeropol]

Overactive, talkative, pressured speech; racing
thoughts, flights of ideas; inflated self-
esteem; need no sleep; easily distracted; judgment
wasted. The Westside wail of words. Steam
pours onto subway platform as crowd hangs back
of turnstile waiting to see if trains will
run. Two feet canary, team fleets of
aquamarine. For all the talk about decentered I's
there's a lot of overbuilt egos. Like
lips passing in the Fright. (We thought

we might be better than.) Beyond any bromide
hidden in assumptions and retarded by lachrymose
perambulation, hollering for benefit when all
the swirl spies pleistocene maquettes. Where
during the time of the observance chortled
aboard a lack, preemptive to detain
maladroit possession, steamed at
what reposed, dishevelled, on a fair
and merry query. As right is as and
just enclosure deeds the doing spun, so
bid departure, fore enamoured, seeds
the sowing sunk. *They* asked me how I knew
a shade of blue was blue; *I*, in tune, re-
plied, when you've got two eyes, folks
return your fire. Hunted down or
hunting. Fabulous forsook, the code without
the signals. And who remembers Leon
Klinghoffer and forgets those with no names
or faces who perish without trace and
less sanction? The Lord looks on
those or these, but, deaf and dumb, gropes
at making signs of solids. Ignominious
restitution, a civilization unable to rise
as high as a gutter; yet kindness
makes fools glow with sedulous light

& the stunted grow incandescent. These
are the words we cannot hear, a language
of sighs. Here are the verbs we have
not curved, vested by sleight: cascade, retort,
vitiate, effloresce. Staccato deserts the ob-
ligato, amounts that turn against, in which
to spread, invaginated prescience before a
nod to cruise: pratfall or billy-
goated & bubbling up like whine.
The world we seek is wiped.
Sitting up, standing,
falling down. & the river turns
to slush & the slush
to shacks but there
is no encampment
& no prognostication for
a sail is a Dot & a
Rot is a shirt
& a lurch
devolves into twin
doves or antiquarian
swans
but more likely a
pigeon.
Clubbed by stupidity

intoxicate of
stupefaction. Coming on like
gangbusters and then just
banging. (We thought
we might be . . .) Alerted,
flushed, remanded to
reminders. "He took so much
disparity," she said. "He was
so grave attending the . . ."
Milkweed
or filched rudders
(rubbers).
The ghost of a semblance of a
dive. Altered, adiabatically foregone.
Rosy-fingered hiccups, polyglot
hibiscus. "At the time, I was troubled
that poets could neither tell readers the name
of the device dispensed nor possible side
effects. Now, if you care to think about
it, even advising a reader to give
aspirin to a fevered child involves a
complicated series of aesthetical and ethical choices."
May philosophers, December social scientists. Having
completed the spadework on the lattice, she
took up, as one might a pair of spectacles, the long-jammed

plan of village of R——, in the county of
P———, professing no more than an historical
interest in a rumored subterranean passage
that connected the village to its
remonstration. Never abandoning fury for curiosity
self-aggrandizement for repulsion. Howevers which
adorn multifoliate pummelling, hung by
plunge and agglutinated with tetradactyls.
Sumptuous sunder (rife with rips). "Sawyer
called it transference, I call it baloney."
Dovetails with
apologia, garlic press. "I'll
tell you this, Sam, you've
got some serious problems that require
professional help." Galvanized
Gargantua, doppler of sudden *zeitgeist*. Sunless
in the sun. For each of us
must decide the level of response
we can afford to give readers in their quest
for truthful, accurate information. Benevolent
deception, partial truths, white lies, and other
forms of circumvention should not be ruled
out. If readers come to us for authoritative guidance,
it is important that we not disappoint them—or they
will turn to other, less reliable, media. "I

just can't hit that number
worth a damn." Garden-
variety effluvium.
When guest is seated, go to door and ring
bell twice. Slow boat to Bayonne, big bust in
Saskatoon. Elementary tuning porch. Who
waves the flaccid flag, downing a silvery
flask, and wrests cacorythmias from
a nest of horns. *Bleat, bleat don't
you know the shoals.* (We thought . . .) Still
the joust has made its recapitulation and the Trout
fills the hall: skies of pomegranates and a
ceiling of guffaws. Along alighted melodies
that . . .
Something there is that doesn't love a
pawn, that wants it smashed, and that its pawning
for. As if
a runner might o'ertake her strife
and patch the lost, unstrap this pediment
of feeling's long and agate train. Much
as you say, to start, at least unconsciously
familiar (usual bulging): but the, we did,
was a, she managed, and how, every time.
Or rolled over, onto something (alchemical
projectile), schmaltzed up with predictable

thrashing. Upstairs for; or is so in the meantime you
can actually precondition, have trouble with, as you—
quote—to absorb roughhouse, endless transfer inflicted
in passing out (but toneless) exoneration. Yesterday
I got, I became, I couldn't understand, I
should be finishing, or some such function as
a viper. Both because and because. Like
the idea of soon, excerpting plans who asked
to duplicate in terms of expanding, since
if, which have been a part of, was news
to me. Weird and Red! Though, for example, they
say 'Baltimore' different in 'Boston'.
Studiously unprepared (oxymoronic
modesty). Like
loss that melts, topical
glaciers make their move. "There's
a bay inside o' Heaven
made of spray, mazed with crape
& it's acommin' for us
couple o' days, aft a long haze."
The antimonophysite heresy: management
refuses responsibility for personal belongings checked
with management. Saucy sailing, bossy
commiseration—before the point is dry.
Fecundly familiar, incontinent supplication.

But not, according to Myron O'Mally; the
bored haberdasher denied any involvement
in the multimillion dollar confidence
confection. Roasting the Host, toasting the boast.
As trippingly entreaties us to linger, where
hushed in the calm of plums, a votive
respirator hums. Humungous desolation, lodged
at flotilla and superannuated fortnightly.
Suppurating bombast (lain along the lane, the
lady lit a Lucky). When I arrived
the reader was lying
flat on the bathroom floor
without any clothes
and complaining of
severe logorrhea. These are
the criteria I have tried to get
out from under
insofar as they would lead to
tighter analogies, less rhetorical
affect. Furthermore, we
are simply miles apart
flatulently wrong
bad bit of deflecting—because you support, on
that topic, no more
about as themes

which well up against this
(tiresome allegation) to
a place like Sovereign Privilege
(sense of from) go in
the direction of, link
constrained.
True I do load
on a spectrum more
than peripheral, and also
more germane as a sweeping,
without swaying. Unbridgeable gulf
by a long shot.
Clear crystal adipose tissue. For
example, yesterday I refused to sell a man
a capon. Mule
of a guy. At dusk,
a dullard's thoughts turn
to dinner. Always
wants what's out of
reach. The search
for nonproverbial language:
child sticks finger
in crank. Suppose
your tooth hurt.
Get dressed, descend the ladder.

(Later.) To be among such constitutive & fibrous
fathers & be so slaphappy. *The world we seek
was swiped.* (We thought we . . .) & rushing
headfirst into the saltmines of the heart. On
the other hand, you can always spend more time
improving your chess. Romanticism is
analogic, modernism is digital. Marxianism
with a tiny middle-class face. "I got
bowls coming out of my ears." "There's
a three-inch opening in the incinerator." &
the Heart of Africa bleeds black blood. Every
day of apartheid dwarfs (every
slash of entitlements mocks)
the grief for
seven dead star warriors. Logic
skates on the brain, reason
weighs
on the mind.
Once
I
saw
a
man
walk
into

a

pole.

"You're like an uncooked nerve."

From amniotic fluid to

semiotic

fluidlessness. Semi-

arctic; infra-

papillary. Semi-idiotic. Semi-automatic

nosedive. Baby

Doc's dead! Death

to all tyrants

who feast

on the misery

of the people!

Illusion or

myth?

When reason swells

with repose then love is scorched

flight.

Some

like it

popped.

"Haiti? Isn't

that where Richard Burton made one of his

movies?" "Every

Jew a .22." Blinking, mumbling
sprawling. "Don't
eat so fast, people will think
you're hungry." Crazy Eddy's
Martin Luther King Day Portable Stereo
Sale. Sondheim
slumped on a sofa in his Manhattan
townhouse. "The important thing isn't
the parties you join but the parties you
make." Or, a shell game's better
than no game. When
the Messiah comes, the rust
will fall from the scales
on our eyes. *Some
like it cracked*. Doubled
over with second guesses.
"Just tell me what you want."
Stove-top denunciations, roving bands of
expectation. For God is
scales not vapor: each day its
dew (a portmanteau in every curlycue).
"I've done everything in my power to make this palatable."
In the priestless churches of San Juan Chamula (the
sentence will not end). Asking,
Where are the Bickfords of yesteryear, where

the Schrafft's? While in the back corridors of time, where
nothing is lost, the crowds swarm Lundy's at Sheepshead
Bay. We (who?) thought to build a diadem
& kicked against the slates by which
each is measure & found wanting what
is ready at hand but grasped too hard.
Better than this puncture's pride at punching, to
find a deck of turns, a float of
tufts, & prattle sightlessly among the chaise-
lit lawns.

CHARLES BERNSTEIN

Born in 1950 in New York City, Charles Bernstein received an undergraduate education at Harvard University. After graduating, he lived in Vancouver, British Columbia and Santa Barbara, where he worked as a technical editor, before returning to New York City. In 1977 he married painter Susan Bee, his editorial and artistic collaborator.

His first book publication, *Parsing*, appeared in 1976. In 1978 he began editing, with Bruce Andrews, the influential critical journal, $L=A=N=G=U=A=G=E$. The title of this journal quickly became a descriptive term to characterize a wide range of American poets whose work, discussed in the journal, focuses on language itself—how language means, how it is structured, how it sounds, and how it looks on the page. Not all of these poets share the same aesthetic, but the term, "Language" poets—for better or worse—stuck and came to be recognized as a major force in American poetics from the 1970s to the present.

The same year, Sun & Moon Press, in its first book publication, published Bernstein's *Shade*, a work that came to characterize his early writing, made of basically short lines that each recontextualize and transform the meaning of the previous and the next. The poetry that results is a work of jumps, leaps, fissures, breaks, and other disjunctive devices that also function together to create a meaningful, and often lyrical, whole.

Two short works, *Poetic Justice* and *Senses of Responsibility*, appeared in 1979, and Bernstein's first collection, *Controlling Interests*, was published the following year in 1980. This book received international critical acclaim and established Bernstein's poetic reputation, which was further solidified with the publication of *Islets/Irritations* in 1983 and with a substantial book of essays in 1985, *Content's Dream*.

The *Sophist*, published in 1987, further extended Bernstein's range, making even more apparent his comic genius and his fascination with pairing radically different syntactical patterns of language with the same poem and volume.

Artifice of Absorption (1987) gave further evidence of Bernstein's critical perspicaciousness. His other books include *Disfrutes* (1981), *The Occurrence of Tune* (1981, a collaboration with Susan Bee), *Stigma* (1981), *Resistance* (1983), and the *Nude Formalism* (1989, again in collaboration with Susan Bee). Bernstein has also translated and edited several periodical anthologies of contemporary poets.

In 1989 Bernstein was appointed to the David Gray Chair at the State University of New York, Buffalo.

Sun & Moon Classics

Sun & Moon Classics is a publicly supported nonprofit program to publish new editions and translations or republications of outstanding world literature of the late nineteenth and twentieth centuries. Organized by The Contemporary Arts Educational Project, Inc., a nonprofit corporation, and published by its program Sun & Moon Press, the series is made possible, in part, by grants and by individual contributions.

This book was made possible, in part, through matching grants from the National Endowment for the Arts, the California Arts Council and through contributions from the following individuals:

William and Genee Fadiman (Bel Air, California)
Rose and Jerry Fox (Pikesville, Maryland)
Perla and Amiram V. Karney (Bel Air, California)
Herbert Lust (Greenwich, Connecticut)
In Memoriam: John Mandanis
Marjorie and Joseph Perloff (Pacific Palisades, California)
Dr. Marvin and Ruth Sackner (Miami Beach, Florida)
Catharine R. Stimpson (Staten Island, New York)

The following individuals serve The Contemporary Arts Educational Project, Inc. as advisors:

David Antin (La Jolla, California)
Paul Auster (Brooklyn, New York)
Charles Bernstein (Buffalo, New York)
Howard N. Fox (Los Angeles, California)
Peter Glassgold (Brooklyn, New York)
Fanny Howe (La Jolla, California)
Nathaniel Mackey (Santa Cruz, California)
Clarence Major (Davis, California)
Ron Padgett (New York, New York)
Marjorie Perloff (Pacific Palisades, California)
Edouard Roditi (Paris, France)
Jerome Rothenberg (Encinitas, California)

Douglas Messerli
Publisher, Sun & Moon Press
Director, The Contemporary Arts Educational Project, Inc.

1. MRS. REYNOLDS, by Gertrude Stein
2. SMOKE AND OTHER EARLY STORIES, by Djuna Barnes
   with an Introduction by Douglas Messerli
3. THE FLAXFIELD, by Stijn Streuvels
   translated from the Dutch by Andre Lefevere and
   Peter Glassgold; with an Introduction by the
   translators
4. PRINCE ISHMAEL, by Marianne Hauser
5. NEW YORK, by Djuna Barnes
   edited with Commentary by Alyce Barry; with a
   Foreword by Douglas Messerli
6. DREAM STORY, by Arthur Schnitzler
   translated from the German by Otto P. Schinnerer
7. THE EUROPE OF TRUSTS, by Susan Howe
   with an Introduction by the author
8. TENDER BUTTONS, by Gertrude Stein
9. DESCRIPTION, by Arkadii Dragomoschenko
   translated from the Russian by Lyn Hejinian and
   Elena Balashova; with an Introduction by Michael
   Molnar
10. SELECTED POEMS: 1963-1973, by David Antin
    with a Foreword by the author
11. MY LIFE, by Lyn Hejinian
12. LET'S MURDER THE MOONSHINE: SELECTED WRITINGS,
    by F. T. Marinetti
    translated from the Italian by R. W. Flint and
    Arthur A. Coppotelli; with an Introduction by R. W.
    Flint; and a Preface by Marjorie Perloff
13. THE DEMONS, by Heimito von Doderer [2 volumes]
    translated from the German by Richard and Clara Winston
14. ROUGH TRADES, by Charles Bernstein

Forthcoming

43 FICTIONS, by Steve Katz
THE ICE PALACE, by Tarjei Vesaas
   translated from the Norwegian by Elizabeth Rokkan

DARK RIDE AND OTHER PLAYS, by Len Jenkin
   with a Statement by Joseph Papp; and an Introduction
   by the author
PIECES 'O SIX, by Jackson Mac Low
   with a Preface by the author; and computer videographics
   by Anne Tardos
NUMBERS AND TEMPERS: SELECTED POEMS 1966-1986, by Ray
   DiPalma
CHILDISH THINGS, by Valery Larbaud
   translated from the French by Catherine Wald
THE CELL, by Lyn Hejinian
AS A MAN GROWS OLDER, by Italo Svevo
   translated from the Italian by Beryl De Zoete; with
   an Introduction by Stanislaus Joyce; and an Essay on
   Svevo by Edouard Roditi
ETERNAL SECTIONS, by Tom Raworth
OWN FACE, by Clark Coolidge